Chronic Christmas
Surviving the Holidays with a Chronic Illness

By Lene Andersen

Visit Lene Andersen's website at www.theseatedview.com

Copy editor: Holly Sawchuk   www.writerrescue.ca
Cover design: Aimee Coveney   www.authordesignstudio.com
Author photo: Sophie Kinachtouk   www.skphotography.ca

Published November, 2016 by Two North Books
www.twonorthbooks.com

Disclaimer:

This book is not intended as a substitute for the medical advice of
physicians. The reader should regularly consult a physician in
matters relating to his/her health. The author is not responsible for
adverse effects or consequences sustained by any person using this
book.

For Laurie Kingston
who was there at the beginning

Welcome to Your Advent Calendar

Christmas is my favorite holiday. I love everything about it. The carols, the shopping, the baking, and wrapping gifts. I love the smell of the pine and fir trees being sold on the corner, and I adore all the vibrant colors brightening up an otherwise drab time of year.

Also the cookies. I'm really fond of Christmas cookies.

This season also has a lot of stress. The lead-in to Christmas can be wonderfully enjoyable, but it's a lot of work. And that goes double when you have a chronic illness.

Living with chronic illness is already a balancing act. It requires a lot of time and attention, and the pain and fatigue affect everything you do.

Then you add Christmas to the mix, and that's when things can get extra wobbly. You want to create a perfect Christmas for the people you love, but the chronic illness demands so much that there isn't enough energy left over. You try to push through anyway, and before you know it you are in pain, exhausted, and not enjoying yourself at all.

Chronic Christmas: Surviving the Holidays with a Chronic Illness is an Advent calendar of tips for a sane holiday season. This book started as a series of posts on my blog, The Seated View (TheSeatedView.com), and they were just aching to become something more. So I used the blog posts as a jumping-off point and added something extra for the people in your life.

Because this is for all of you. Your family and friends often want to help but may not know what you need. And maybe you are feeling too overwhelmed or reticent to ask for what would be the most helpful. This book gives you all ideas for how to bridge the gap.

Each chapter will start out with a section dedicated to you, the reader who has a chronic illness, sharing something you can do to help yourself enjoy the season. And then there will be another section for those who'd like to help you, with some tips along the same theme.

I've also added a few surprises every now and again. I am not going to tell you what or where they are, though. Surprises are part of what makes Christmas so delicious.

You don't have to do every one of the tips in all of the chapters. I suspect that would be exhausting and the very opposite of what Chronic Christmas is about. Find what speaks to you. Dive into that and let the rest slide. This is your book now, and you get to decide how you want to use it.

I'd love to hear which tips you like and which ones you use. You can get in touch with me via email at lene@yourlifewithra.com. On social media, look for @theseatedview on Twitter and Instagram. On Facebook, you can find me at www.facebook.com/LeneAndersenwriter.

If you share photos of your adventures during the holiday season, use the hashtag #ChronicChristmas. I can't wait for all of you who followed along in this book to show each other what you have done (or not done).

Creating this Advent calendar was a lot of fun, and it helped me get into the Christmas spirit. I hope it does the same for you.

Lene.

December 1st
Shop Online

Why not do your gift shopping online?

Cyber Monday may have been a mere few days ago, but there are still deals to be had. One of the best parts of doing your shopping on the Internet is that the poking about you normally do on the web now has a purpose. Procrastinating? Wasting time? Not at all! You are on the hunt for the perfect gifts for your loved ones.

Online shopping is God's gift to people with a chronic illness. Okay, so maybe it's a gift from geeks, but it works either way. You don't have to leave the house, you don't have to march through the mall, you don't have to battle the crowds. You can shop in your PJs and at 3 a.m. if you have painsomnia (what the chronic pain community calls insomnia due to pain). In that case, online shopping is also a coping mechanism. It's wonderfully distracting.

Although I'm a big fan of getting ahead of the problem, don't rush to finish all of your shopping in the next day or two. Most of the larger retailers offer very quick shipping, often for free if you spend a certain amount. Before you place your orders, spend some time looking around to find just the right thing for the people on your list.

You may also want to make a mental note to start a gift list document on your computer for next year. I've done this for a long time. Whenever I stumble upon something nifty that makes me think of a friend or family member, I add the link to the gift list. By the time their birthday or the next holiday season rolls around, all I need to do is open the document and decide which item I want to get for them. This kind of treasure trove of potential presents is a gift to yourself that keeps on giving, saving you energy throughout the year.

And it has an additional benefit. Because you're putting together the list over time when you see something truly interesting, you'll be a star whenever there is a gift-giving opportunity. Instead of settling on something that's only vaguely relevant to the recipient, you will always knock it out of the park.

Helping Someone with a Chronic Illness

Malls are a bit of a nightmare for anyone at this time of the year. But for people with chronic illness, going to the mall during the holiday season can exhaust them to the point of needing several days to recover. Walking long distances while carrying packages and standing in long lines can cause pain and extreme fatigue. And then there is navigating stores inundated with "festive" scents, sure to trigger migraines or asthma attacks.

Although your friend or family member may be doing most of their shopping online, there are always items that need to be picked up from a store. Offer to help out by shopping with or for them.

Having someone along for company while shopping can be a huge help for the person who has a chronic illness. Do the driving if you can – it can save your friend some much-needed energy. When you get to the mall, make a plan of attack that involves the least amount of walking. Then carry coats and packages and take their place in line while they take a rest on a bench. Don't forget to make time for a decadent snack or nice lunch for the two of you.

Potentially even better than accompanying your friend is leaving them at home to rest while you head to the mall with their list. I don't know anyone who wouldn't love to have a personal shopper. This can be a very meaningful gift to someone you know who lives with chronic illness.

While we are talking about presents, there's one more thing you can do: help wrap them! Wrapping can be difficult for people who have conditions that may cause pain or affect the dexterity in their hands. Light some candles, and enjoy a glass of wine or some hot chocolate and some seasonal treats. Then let the wrapping paper, tape, and tags fly! There's work involved, but it is also a wonderful way of spending a bit of quiet time with someone you love during this busy season.

Chronic Christmas

December 2nd
Pace Yourself When Eating

Pace yourself with the goodies.

This is the season of chocolate, cookies, fudge, fruitcake (undeservedly maligned), and more chocolate. While we're at it, let's have a little drink, shall we?

There's nothing wrong with indulging – after all, there are lots of really yummy foods available this month. Part of what makes the holiday season so special is the custom of making certain foods and sweets only once a year. As we continue the holiday traditions of our parents and grandparents, full-sensory memories of childhood rush in when we take a bite of that cookie or taste that side dish for the Christmas meal.

Marcel Proust wrote about this phenomenon in *Remembrance of Things Past*. He spun out a memory triggered by the exquisite joy brought forth by a taste of a madeleine (a small cake) into a really, really long book. I haven't read it, but I love the story behind it.

It would be a shame to deny yourself the opportunity to enjoy those fond memories or simply to partake of all the delicious foods available during the season. And you don't have to miss out.

But moderation is key. Instead of five pieces of chocolate, maybe stick to one (okay, two). Instead of four glasses of eggnog, have one per occasion and drink sparkling water or tea for the rest of the evening. And so on. You won't feel deprived. And you won't stand out as that one person who's nibbling on a lettuce leaf, making the other guests feel bad for scarfing down everything in sight.

This suggestion is not to help you stay thin through the holidays – a little extra padding will only help keep you warm this winter. It's simply intended for you to feel better. Some people with chronic illness and chronic pain find that sugar and rich foods can be triggers for increased symptoms. Who needs that, especially during the festive season? Using moderation with the goodies is one way you can keep pain and other symptoms in check, helping yourself to get through this month in one piece.

Helping Someone with a Chronic Illness

By no means are you expected to be the food police, snatching treats out of the mouths of your friends and family members who have chronic illnesses. It would be exhausting and obnoxious, so best not to go there. It would probably also be best not to make remarks such as "are you sure you should be eating that?" or "is that really included in your diet?" Saying such things only risks having the dish in question thrown at you.

A better way to be respectful of your friend who might be on a special diet is to check with them before you decide on the menu for your holiday event. This is actually a good idea whether you are inviting someone who you know has a chronic illness or all of your guests seem to be as healthy as a herd of horses. Food allergies and intolerances are becoming more common. As well, many people follow a variety of special diets ranging from Paleo to being vegan. Occasionally, it can be a bit of a challenge to have people over for a meal.

It can also be difficult to be a guest when there isn't a thorough understanding that getting even a bit of a trigger food can make you sick for days. As well, don't we all know a vegetarian or vegan who's fed up with being presented with yet another salad?

So why not do a potluck? Everyone who is invited brings a dish or some snacks, and don't forget to assign drinkables, plates, and utensils to one of the guests. In my family, we like to gather a large group of people together a couple of times a year for a potluck, making sure everyone is aware of allergies and food intolerances. This makes it less of a financial burden for the person who is hosting. It also makes for an exciting selection of food when everyone brings something special.

Chronic Christmas

December 3rd
Decorate Five Minutes Every Day

When I look at the beautifully decorated homes in magazines, on blogs, and in the movies, I wish I had the energy to do more. It would be nice if my home could evoke the uniquely seasonal coziness that helps create the spirit of Christmas.

I also wish Lucy the Cat didn't have an obsession with eating pine and climbing trees, but that's beside the point.

The solution to the former is to apply the five-minute rule. No matter how busy or tired you feel, chances are that most days you can do your task of choice for five minutes. It may not sound like much, but it's amazing how quickly that bit of time from yesterday, today, tomorrow, and the next day add up and work together to create something real.

It does so in the same way that a thousand small puzzle pieces can make a picture, or tens of thousands of individual knitting stitches can make a pair of mittens. They get accomplished by setting aside a bit of time every day to gradually do a big task. You can use this system to keep your house clean, build muscles to make you stronger, or decorate your home for Christmas.

Start in the room where you spend the most time. Perhaps that's your living room, your kitchen, or your family room. If that one room is the only area you decorate, surround yourself with Christmas spirit. Add festive strings of lights, especially if you live in an area where it gets dark early near the holidays.

Think about candles, too. To me, there is nothing quite like candlelight in the depth of winter.

If you have it in you, widen the circle of decorating madness to a second area in your home. You started with bringing Christmas cheer to yourself. Now think about bringing Christmas to where your holiday guests will be. Then, if you have more energy, choose a third room and so on. If you start today, your home will begin to look beautiful in a week, and might be done two weeks from now.

Sure, your Christmas decoration boxes will be on display in the living room until you work your way to the bottom. But unless you're having the queen over for dinner, what does it matter?

I do recommend that you close the box firmly in between decorating sessions. Especially if you have a pet that's anything like Lucy.

Helping Someone with a Chronic Illness

I bet that deep down inside – or maybe not so deep down – there's a part of you that would love being Santa's Little Helper. How enticing to be part of creating the magic of the Christmas spirit! As a child, you may have wanted to visit Santa's workshop. As an adult, you can help bring the magic to the home of someone who can't do it on their own.

Make a date with that person you know who has a chronic illness and descend upon them wearing a Santa hat and carrying gingerbread and mulled wine. Or the fixings for hot chocolate if you want to keep the occasion non-alcoholic and the decorations reasonably straight.

Let the person you care about take the lead. If they are up for actively participating, the two of you can work together, with you doing the more physically intense tasks. Take frequent breaks to enjoy the refreshments you brought.

If the person whom you're helping is having a really bad day or has serious pain or mobility limitations, you may want to put them in the captain's chair (so to speak). Let them direct as you do all or most of the work. It might also be a good idea to split the festivities over a couple of days.

Because I can't decorate myself, I get help from a friend or one of my attendants every December. As long as you put a bit of thought and organization into it, it's quite easy. Also unexpectedly hilarious, as you figure out how to work together. It can be especially helpful for both of you to let go of the need for perfection.

As well, you should get your idea of how things should look out of the way. After all, this is your friend's home you're decorating, not your own. If they want to include a live reindeer in their nativity tableau, it's up to them. And potentially the animal licensing department.

Chronic Christmas

December 4th
Take a Walk

Is it cold out? Is it raining? Better yet, is it snowing?

Take a walk, and bring an umbrella if there is wet stuff coming from above. Moving will get you out of your head and into your body, which is a good thing when you have a chronic illness. It helps you connect the two and find out that they actually do work together, even if there are occasional hiccups.

Moving around outside has a number of benefits. It exposes you to fresh air (yes, even in big cities). It also makes your doctor happy and less likely to go on about physical activity.

But more importantly, it gets you out of the house.

Look! There are other people in the world! Your neighbors have put up lights, and there are Christmas trees lined up in front of the stores. Inhale that wonderful scent of pine as deeply as you can.

Well, perhaps not if you have bad asthma, but I trust you to adjust as needed.

Likewise, make sure that your walk is safe. If your legs are affected by your chronic illness, you may want to consider getting a cane, especially on days when it is wet or slippery. I can see you cringing at the thought, but remember that a cane is not a symbol of giving up or giving in. It is just a tool to help you get out of the house. These days, you can even get some snazzy designs. If the thought of a cane is more than you can bear, you might want to consider getting some trekking poles. They provide support and make you look like a mountaineer to boot.

Make your walk long or short, whatever feels good to you, and then go home to curl your hands around a warm cup of tea. Or a cold glass of lemonade, if you live in the southern hemisphere. And then feel the spirit of the season settle in.

Helping Someone with a Chronic Illness

We live in a sedentary culture. Unless you visit the gym every day – and not many of us do – chances are you don't move nearly enough. And neither do I, or your neighbor, or your coworkers.

The good news is that you don't have to join the gym or run marathons to improve your fitness. Taking a walk is an excellent start, so why not do it with someone you know who has a chronic illness? Setting up a buddy system can be a huge help no matter what you do, be it walking, dieting, writing, or any other task that requires perseverance and motivation. Knowing that you're relying on each other to get out of the house makes it much harder to give in to the siren call of watching Netflix on the couch.

Find out which kind of limitations your friend, neighbor, or family member has because of their chronic illness and adapt your walking to that. This could mean walking a shorter distance and/or doing it slowly. You may also need to adjust the time of day that you walk. For instance, if your friend is sensitive to heat, bright sunlight, or humidity, walking in the evening after the sun goes down is less likely to make their chronic illness flare (an increase in symptoms). Have a conversation about what you both would like to do and the aspects of your lives that affect how and when you walk.

You might also want to bring the kids. Just like grown-ups, kids lead increasingly sedentary lives. Experts recommend that you teach kids healthy habits that involve being physically active. The bonus to walking with children is that there are no competing interests, such as video games or telephones. Because you will all be leaving your mobile phones at home, right? This creates an opportunity for conversation between adults and children and can help you be more in tune with what's going on in your kids' lives.

And by the way… you will absolutely be forgiven if you want to leave the kids at home with your spouse while you enjoy some grown-up time alone with your friend.

Chronic Christmas

December 5th
Focus In

There is no such thing as "less is more" during the holiday season. Although there is the odd minimalist, most of us believe in throwing more decorations on the inside of the house and more lights on the outside. One of my favorite holiday traditions is checking out the elaborate light shows that dot the neighborhood with moving lights, snowmen, and Santa and his reindeer. I love the way so many people embrace my dad's favorite homemade saying that "more is better."

More can also be a little overwhelming, especially when your body is resisting all attempts to be festive. And before you know it, in enter The Shoulds. You *should* have a big tree, elaborately decorated. You *should* host your entire extended family for Christmas dinner. You *should* knit the traditional ugly Christmas sweater for each of your children. Once The Shoulds sneak into your mind, guilt quickly follows.

So why not redefine what festive is to you? Go for less, but not in a minimalist way (unless that floats your boat). Instead make what you do count. Think about what makes you really happy, what is quintessentially Christmas to you. And then do that to the best of your ability. Do it with abandon, do it to the max.

If it's a wreath on your door, buy the most beautiful wreath you can find. Or maybe make one yourself. If it's your grandmother's snickerdoodle cookies, make that the one cookie you bake this season and make lots of them.

Maybe instead of traipsing around to several holiday parties, you and your friends get together for one event, such as a slightly boozy crafty evening at which you all create increasingly imperfect decorations. Make some glögg, a warm spiced wine traditional in the Scandinavian countries, and proudly display the aforementioned imperfect decorations. Don't forget to have alcohol-free refreshments as well, for designated drivers and people who don't partake.

It doesn't matter what tradition you choose, because it is the holidays in a nutshell. Shed whatever guilt you might feel about everything you don't do. Embrace and enjoy the moments you choose to have.

The Andersen Family Glögg Recipe

Glögg is a spiced wine popular in Scandinavia during the Christmas season. Everyone develops their own unique variation, so approach this with a sense of adventure and never mind strict measurements. Because there aren't any. Taste it as you go along and, with a bit of practice, you'll create your own version.

One note: this is delicious and doesn't taste like alcohol, so it's easy to get a bit too much. Make sure there are designated drivers or enough money for cabs, especially if you go for the more potent version.

Ingredients

Red wine, enough for two moderate glasses per person. It doesn't have to be fancy – all the other flavors will drown out any fine undertones in the wine.

Brandy (optional)

Danish akvavit or other unflavored schnapps (optional)

1 tablespoon or so whole cloves per bottle of wine

7 cinnamon sticks or so per bottle of wine

Raisins, a handful or two, depending on preference

Blanched, chopped almonds, 1-2 handfuls, depending on preference

A bit of sugar (optional)

Get a pot that's big enough to hold all the ingredients and pour in the red wine. Heat on the stove at medium, enough to simmer but not to boil. If you're making the really grown-up version, add brandy and schnapps. Be conservative – you can always add more.

Add cloves, cinnamon sticks, raisins, sugar, and almonds. Note: the almonds are the most delicious when they've been stewing in the concoction, absorbing the wine and getting a bit soft. However, if any of your guests are allergic to nuts, serve the almonds separately so those who are not allergic can add them to their glasses.

Let simmer 30 minutes or more to allow all of the delicious flavors to blend. Keep on the stove at minimum heat, so it stays warm between servings.

Serve in a mug with a teaspoon so your guests can munch on the almonds and raisins. If you have silver spoons, you may want to try serving the traditional way, in glögg glasses, if you have them. They may be available at IKEA, but any type of smallish glass for hot tea will also work just fine. According to my mother, the silver spoons are essential to prevent the hot liquid from cracking the glasses. Mugs are fine too, and you can use regular spoons to eat the delicious blend of almonds and raisins. Just keep a bit of an eye on how many drinks your guests have. Glögg can have a significant kick.

In Denmark, glögg parties traditionally feature æbleskiver, a fried, sweet sort of dumpling dipped in sugar and jam. And it's no coincidence. It's a pretty heavy treat that can nicely absorb the alcohol. When you plan the munchables, don't go too light on the snacks – anything with carbs that can act as a balance will be ideal.

Helping Someone with a Chronic Illness

I'm pretty sure you've also been reading the sections for people who live with chronic illness. After all, you are a concerned friend or family member who wants to help – if you didn't, you wouldn't be reading this book.

I don't mean to lay a guilt trip on you if you haven't been reading those other sections. The reason I'm mentioning this is that I'm also pretty sure that as you read the above, a wistful feeling snuck into your heart. Wouldn't it be great to not go all out this year? How would it feel to actually have time to celebrate the holiday season with the people you love instead of running around like a chicken with its head cut off, trying to cater to The Shoulds?

Feeling overwhelmed and guilty about everything you can't do is an experience shared by almost everyone during the holiday season. It's one way you can build bridges between people who live with chronic illness and their healthy peers.

So maybe you're the person who gets the ball rolling. Talk to friends and family about doing less so you can do more of what you really love about the holidays. If there are more of you doing this, it's a lot easier for the person who has a chronic illness to focus in without guilt or depression. Together, you can offer each other support as you buck tradition and focus in instead of going all out.

And maybe you're the one who offers up your home to host that crafty evening. That doesn't mean that it all falls to you. You might make the glögg because your stove is right there. But it's only fair that the responsibility for bringing treats and craft supplies is distributed among your guests. (I don't have to mention the designated driver thing again, do I?)

And then enjoy yourself.

Chronic Christmas

December 6th
Throw Money at the Problem

Were you enthusiastically getting behind my suggestion to focus in, as I mentioned in the last chapter? Then chances are that the holidays have become a problem instead of a celebration to you. That's a sure sign you need a holiday intervention.

Okay, this is not a full-fledged intervention but one in which you grab yourself by the scruff of the neck (metaphorically, not literally, because *ouch*), give yourself a shake, and... throw money at the problem.

As much as you can, buy your way out of whatever feels like work instead of joyful preparation. You can hire people to wrap presents for you. If you're not averse to a little child labor, enlist your kids in this. They get to make a bit of extra money, you get to sit on the couch and direct, and being co-conspirators in keeping the gifts secret can be a bonding experience.

The same goes for pretty much anything else about holiday preparation. If you're hosting a Christmas party – perhaps as your one thing in your quest to focus in – you don't need to make the food. There are some very nice elves at the supermarket who will do it for you. The in-depth cleaning before everyone comes over? Call a cleaning service. Their staff will happily put on a Santa hat and make your home sparkle.

"That would be awesome if I had the money," you say. Living with a chronic illness means a lot of extra expenses.

Throwing money at the problem can be a challenge if finances are tight. But there are ways around that.

You do some bartering with friends. For instance, they help you now and you help them with their taxes in April. You may not be a financial whiz, but you have other skills they could use. Maybe you are a brilliant organizer and can help them get a handle on a pile of papers. Or perhaps you're highly skilled with a search engine and can locate that hard-to-find antique book they've wanted for years. You could also take them up on that offer of help they gave you that you've felt too awkward to accept. Give them plenty of notice that you need a hand, though. It's a nice thing to do.

It's not who does the cleaning or wrapping or baking that matters. What matters is that you are well enough to enjoy the holidays with your family. That's the best gift you can give them. And yourself.

Helping Someone with a Chronic Illness

Let's face it: children are the only ones for whom the holidays are uncomplicated fun and joy. Once you become an adult, this season involves a lot of work as you do your best to make it special for your kids and the grown-up people you love.

If one of those people is someone who has a chronic illness, they will be feeling the stress of the holiday workload even more. Getting through the day with a chronic illness requires a lot of extra energy. There are tasks that healthy people don't have to do – multiple doctors' appointments, medical tests, wrangling insurance companies. And then there's the fact that everyday tasks take more energy when you're in pain.

Your offer of help can do wonders. Not that elusive some day in the future that never really happens kind of help, but now. This month. Don't say, "Can I help?" Instead say, "I'm setting aside a day to help you before Christmas. When would you like me to come over, and what would you like me to do?"

I'm not saying this because I'm a control freak and trying to script your interactions. It can be difficult for someone who has a chronic illness to think of something when others offer to help. If you have kids, think back to when they were newborns and how much easier it was when someone offered a concrete task.

Staying within the theme of today, you don't have to throw your money at someone else's problem. That is, unless you have money to spare. In that case, an early Christmas present of a cleaning crew will always be welcome by pretty much anyone. And especially by a friend who lives with chronic illness. If your finances are tight as well, giving the gift of yourself can be even more meaningful. Just as you could help decorate, designating yourself as temporary staff can be a miraculous gift. Think one-person cleaning crew, chef to cook a nice meal, or snow shoveler.

Chronic Christmas

December 7th
Use Reindeer (or Technology) for Cards

It usually starts the week before Thanksgiving. First there is a trickle, then a flood. Colored envelopes in red, green, and cream, beautifully addressed and sporting seasonal stamps and stickers, make it clear. The holidays have arrived.

The thought of writing a mountain of cards and addressing a comparable mountain of envelopes, then licking them shut and slapping a stamp on them can make your entire body ache in protest. Signing piles of Christmas cards is enough to give anyone a cramp. When you have a chronic illness, this part of the holiday preparations can lead to pain and a strong desire to create ice pack mittens for your aching hands.

So don't do it.

The Internet is a wonderful thing, making so many parts of our lives easier and more entertaining. Buying gifts online saves you energy for other things, but don't use it on cards. Instead, embrace the e-card! It's much easier on your hands, saves you money, and is good for the environment.

And this time of year, they are specially delivered by Santa's reindeer. Really.

There are oodles of sites that enable you to send an e-card. One of my favorites is Jacquie Lawson's, featuring beautiful English countryside scenes set to lovely music. Receiving one of these cards always feels like an occasion. I should mention that they didn't make me say it – I'm just a happy customer. There is a small annual subscription fee, but you can send as many cards as you want over the year.

If your style is different or you don't want to pay the subscription fee, ask your friend Google to find you "free e-cards." It will give you an embarrassment of riches from which to choose.

And now I'm going to contradict myself. Although e-cards are wonderful, there are a small handful of people to whom I send a real physical card. Older relatives, those on my list who don't have a computer, and people whom I love deeply. Because I'm not sending out a mountain, it's easier to make a bit of a production out of a few cards. I like to make them extra meaningful by creating my own. This isn't nearly as labor-intensive as you'd think.

How to Create Your Own Cards

Making your own cards is simple, especially if you have a digital camera or smartphone. Again, the Internet comes to your rescue. Sites that enable you to make your own products are easy to use – you don't have to be comfortable with graphic design to create something beautiful.

Take a look at your photos and choose the best ones. If you have kids, they are an excellent choice of subject – often the people you love are pretty crazy about your children. Your pet also makes a great subject, as do nature and landscapes.

Once you've created an account on the site of your choosing, upload your photos and use them to make your cards. The sites provide templates for postcards, notecards, and larger cards. You pick the ones you want, insert your photos and perhaps some text, and then you're done!

Once you've created the cards, place your order. Your cards are printed and mailed to you.

I'd recommend that you start as early as possible. It can take a while before you get the cards, especially during the holiday season when there are a lot of orders.

Helping Someone with a Chronic Illness

Who doesn't like to get mail? By which I mean real mail – not flyers or bills. Those we can do without. But not a lot of people seem to like to produce the real mail that we all love so much. This is where you can be super helpful to someone who has a chronic illness and who might have trouble writing. Especially with that mountain of cards that we send out this time of year.

The first thing you can do to help the person is to make a mutual agreement not to send them to each other. Instead spend some time together, either in person (and perhaps use that time to help them in some way or another) or have a nice long talk on the phone.

If your friend or family member very much wants to send out real cards (as opposed to e-cards), you can help with that, too. Perhaps suggest that they put together a holiday letter – you know the type. This can be photocopied and included in every card and then all they have to do is sign the card itself. Well, the envelopes do need to be addressed and stamped, but that could be your job.

Another way you can help is by acting as your friend's hands. If they'd like to write a holiday letter, they might appreciate your help in doing the typing. If they want to design their own card and you have a bit of technical or design know-how, you'd be the perfect person for this task. Find out what kind of style they like and sit next to each other, creating together. Follow their lead – you are acting as their hands, which means you are designing what they would do themselves if they could.

Once all the cards are done, don't forget to take them to the mailbox. This can save your friend or family member some valuable energy that they can use for something else.

December 8th
Say Hello

Living with chronic illness can be profoundly isolating. You may be feeling too crabby to leave the house. When you are out and about, that may take all your energy, causing you to block out the world. Seeing other people takes stamina, and when you have limited reserves, it can be put on the list of things to do when you feel better. The problem with this is that isolating yourself can feed depression. Although connecting with others takes energy, it can also give back. It's much like installing new batteries, reminding you that you're part of a greater community.

So let's do an experiment today.

Instead of looking down or turning inward, instead of being glued to your phone or book, instead of blocking out the world by popping in the earbuds and listening to music, leave it all in your pocket or bag. And look up.

Look at the scenery as you drive by. I should clarify that if you are at the wheel, the only scenery you should be looking at is the road and the traffic. I want you to arrive safely. But if you're lucky enough to be a passenger or public transit user, look out the window. If it's a sunny day, admire the play of shadows on snow.

Look at the crowds. If you're in a public area, take a seat on a bench with a cup of something yummy and a muffin and tune in. People watching is one of the great joys of life. It's even more fun if you combine it with making up stories about the people you see.

Say hello. Strike up a conversation with the person next to you. Share a personal moment with the barista who makes your coffee. Say something nice to a harried sales clerk. Share a bagel and a word with the homeless guy on the corner who is ignored by everyone else.

Engage. Connect. You won't regret it.

Helping Someone with a Chronic Illness

Feeling isolated isn't just something that happens when you have a chronic illness. The stress of everyday life can be exhausting. When you're tired, you turn inwards. Crowds and roads and a long list of things to do can just be too much to take. But just like your family member or friend who has a chronic illness, isolating yourself and disconnecting from others can actually make you feel worse.

So join in the experiment. Take a drive with your friend, and say hello to the world. Try to go to a place where you are surrounded by nature – it can make it easier to open up. It's also a lot prettier in winter than city streets. Take a walk in a park, on a forest trail, or on suburban streets. Listen to the crunch of snow under your boots. Open the windows in the car and breathe in the cold, crisp air. Or not, if you live in a warm area. Look at Christmas decorations, and tell each other which ones you like best.

Take each other out for that cup of something delicious and a muffin. Grab a table at the coffee shop or in the food court and watch people go by. Tell each other stories about them and make your tales fabulous and entertaining. Nothing negative –

you never know who can hear you, and the positive angle is more likely to make everyone feel good.

Chat with each other, but reach out to others as well. The people at the next table, a sales clerk, a security guard. Slow down, take the time, exchange a few words. You could very well make their day and you might meet someone really interesting.

If the two of you can't get together, make a pact to look at the world and the people in it. Then call each other at the end of the day and talk about what you saw and what you thought.

Make a habit of doing this on a regular basis. The more you look, the more you will notice. Taking those moments to connect and engage is an excellent way of coping with stress. It will make you both feel happier.

Chronic Christmas

December 9th
Build a Snowman

Is there snow on the ground? Even a little bit? Then get out there and build a snowman!

Of course, there is no need to get all label-y. Snow person. Or, should you wish to get creative, a snow unicorn, an icy sand castle, or an igloo.

The point is to revisit your childhood. To go back to a snowy afternoon when your mom bundled you up and told you to go outside and play. To remember trying to catch snowflakes, standing with your head thrown back and your tongue out in the cold air. To making snow angels, having a snowball fight, and sharing secrets with a friend in the snow fort you'd just built. If you are having trouble connecting to the playful side of you, make sure to include your kids. There is nothing better to help you disconnect from grown-up responsibility and just laugh. If you don't have children, borrow some from a friend or neighbor.

Then come back inside covered in snow, with your cheeks as red as apples from the cold.

On the day of the first snow, my mom would always make homemade hot chocolate and delicious buns, and we'd warm up from the inside after playing.

Admittedly, the lead-in to this chapter was very much focused on a northern experience. It's entirely likely that a fair number of you who are reading this live in the South, or maybe even all the way south of the equator. Your experience of this time of year is therefore completely different. The idea remains the same though. Remember what you did as a child when your parents told you to get out of the house to get some fresh air.

Snow might be hard to come by at this particular point in time, and not just for those of you who live in southern parts of the world. El Niño and climate change are messing with our ability to bask in the white stuff, but there are so many other ways to have fun.

If it's windy, you can fly a kite. If you're up for it, toss a ball around with your kids or your dog. Ignore the dirt and slobber – it's all part of the experience. If you're having a crappy day, stay inside and color or play a board game.

C'mon, let's go and play.

Helping Someone Who Has a Chronic Illness

When is the last time you played? Truly played, rather than just entertained your kids until they got tired?

Play is about abandon and joy, about laughing so hard that your stomach hurts. It's about letting go of stress and worries and the things you should be doing and just having pure fun. Which doesn't often happen when you're a grown up.

And this is where having a friend or family member who has a chronic illness can work for you!

Start off with a conversation about your favorite memories from childhood. Then recreate them. If you live in an area that has even a smidgen of snow, make the most of it. Make a snow person. If you don't have a lot of snow, make several tiny snowmen. Erm, snow people.

Oh, you know what I mean.

If your friend or family member is having a really hard time with physical activity, bring the snow to them. Maybe dump a couple of handfuls over their head. I can tell you from personal experience that it's pretty fun. You can also put them in charge of the decorations to make the face on this new creation. Or maybe they can give you directions from the porch.

If it's too cold or there is no snow or leaving the house will be too much, play cards or games. Something really silly. Bring some balloons and suck the helium to sound like chipmunks. I don't know anyone who doesn't dissolve into laughter when that happens. Just remember to choose another activity if you or your friend is allergic to latex.

And when your cheeks are as red as apples from the cold, your stomachs hurt from laughing, and you haven't thought of what you ought to be doing for hours, it's time. Indulge yourselves with your favorite childhood treat.

C'mon. Go and play.

Chronic Christmas

December 10th
Embrace Your Inner Dane

Denmark, the country of my birth and childhood, excels at Christmas. It's located far enough north that there is very little daylight during the month of December. What we lack outside, we make up for inside. Every home is strewn with cutout hearts and paper elves lining shelves and any other area where there's space. We stick whole cloves in navel oranges and hang them in the windows with red silk ribbons, where they make the room smell amazing. And we get together with friends and colleagues for wonderful long Christmas lunches. The whole country embraces hygge.

Embraces what??

Hygge, pronounced *hue-gah*, is a Danish term that's hard to explain precisely. Cozy gets part of the way there, but not entirely. Hygge is also about intimacy, trust, love, being comfortable with where you are and whom you're with. It often involves good food, having wonderful, supportive conversations, and there is almost always candlelight. It's nothing short of magical.

On the website for the book *The Danish Way of Parenting*, hygge is described like this: "… it isn't only because of the candles, the nice food and the cozy atmosphere. Hygge is about something much deeper. It is about the power of presence and *really* connecting to others in a drama free way. It is focusing on what is really important – *being* together."

Sounds good, doesn't it?

In Denmark, December is prime hygge time because of the increase in togetherness, yummy food, and – yes, you guessed it – candlelight. Despite the busyness of the season, it's quite common for Danish people to be remarkably stress-free leading up to Christmas.

I bet that's not a coincidence. Hygge is the best de-stresser I've ever come across.

So why not take some time at the end of a busy day to light some candles, gather people you care about – family, friends, maybe your neighbors – and enjoy some food together? Potluck is perfect. Connect to your inner Dane. It might take a bit of practice, but it's the kind of practice you'll love. Quite likely, you'll find that hygge is a natural impulse. Enjoy it.

It's good for the soul.

Helping Someone with a Chronic Illness

You may have noticed a trend in the preceding chapters of this book. Whenever I've talked about you helping someone who has a chronic illness, it has always included the two of you enjoying yourselves while you are helping them. That's because I'm Danish and hygge is ingrained in my DNA.

Hygge is good for the soul, making you feel connected and loved. It helps you let go of stress and recharges your emotional batteries.

Although it is possible to practice hygge on your own, it is even better with company. And that's a real stumbling block for people who live with chronic illness. When they barely have enough energy to make it through the day, creating an evening full of warmth, good food, and love for the people they care about is simply not going to happen.

And that's where you come in.

You likely have people in common with the person you'd like to help. You may be from the same family, or perhaps you have friends or neighbors in common. Volunteer to be a sort of shadow host for your friend. Talk the invitation list out between the two of you – keep it small, no more than 6-8 people, including the two of you and your spouses.

The get-together (very definitely not a party) should be at your friend's house. After all, they are the official host. However, you will do the more physical host duties. This includes cleaning up and creating a warm and inviting atmosphere. Electric lights should be low, with plenty of candles. Don't forget to make them unscented, just in case someone in the group is sensitive to fragrance.

Food is important to creating hygge, but it doesn't need to be elaborate. Start with a couple of bottles of wine (as well as non-alcoholic beverages). Then add some nice cheeses and dips, interesting crackers, and a variety of olives and grapes. This will do the trick just nicely. If wine and cheese are likely to trigger migraines for any of your guests, make sure to provide alternatives.

Once everyone arrives, take a bit of a back seat and let your friend shine as host. It's one of the best gifts you can give to someone who doesn't often get to entertain.

Encourage the guests to sit down in comfortable furniture around a central table that holds the refreshments. You'll find this makes the conversation flow nicely. And it helps everyone to connect in a much warmer and more authentic way than when standing around balancing crackers and a glass of wine.

Don't forget the last part of being a host. Stay long enough to help your friend wash the dishes and clean up.

December 11th
Keep It Reasonable

This is not the first chapter in which I've mentioned the exuberance of the holiday season. It's about going all out and the very opposite of laid back. And really, it's too much for anyone, chronic illness or not.

So pace yourself – not just with eating or traditions but also with the multitude of celebrations. This is the season for parties, lunches, neighborhood drop-ins, office events, and why not squeeze in a couple of brunches as well. It feels absolutely necessary to see everyone, attend every event, and pack it all into four weeks.

And when you have a chronic illness, doing it all is a virtual guarantee that you will spend the actual holidays curled up on your couch in a world of hurt.

So make choices. Healthy and somewhat ruthless choices. This is about balancing where you want to be with getting the most bang for your buck – the buck in this case being your presence. If the host is your dearest friend, it may very well be a command performance. It could also be the one party you can actually miss, because they will understand. Truly understand, not just say so while seething inwardly.

If it's a swanky do put on by your employer, it's probably politically wise to go. It's also the kind of party where you can make an appearance, connect with a few important people, and leave after a decent time. At this kind of event, you can trot out the classic excuse of couldn't-get-a-babysitter or the actual truth: not feeling well. It is important to show up but less important to stay for the entire thing.

And then there's the actual hosting of your family's party on The Big Day. The one that normally falls to you. Perhaps this is the year you discuss taking turns or changing the whole event into a potluck. In my family, the middle-aged generation has taken over the cooking, while my mother (aka the Andersen Matriarch) directs the troops from a comfy chair. Because she can't quite let go.

Some people will be upset if you don't show or if you leave early. Explain as best you can, but don't get guilted into doing something that isn't right for you. This is about your survival, about you being able to be there for your children, for your family. And that's more important than pleasing others.

Helping Someone with a Chronic Illness

Pace yourself.

Oh, if only. How many of us have wanted to bow out of the drinks party on a Thursday evening or grumbled while putting on our finery for the fancy office party? All of us, that's who. There is so much going on in the month between Thanksgiving and Christmas that it would be a blessing to be able to get back an evening, an afternoon, or a Sunday morning.

If you did, you could use it to relax a bit among all the running around. Or maybe get something done that otherwise would be haunting you until you had to stay up much past your bedtime to get it done.

For the member of your family or circle of friends who has a chronic illness, that time could be so valuable for regaining a bit of energy. Or, like you, for getting something done that has been hanging over their head.

There are a couple of ways you can help your friend take care of their chronic illness rather than other people's need for parties. If you're having a holiday event, invite your friend. Make it clear to them that if they need to stay in, practice self-care so they can survive the season, or save up energy for their boss's party, it's okay to skip yours. One of the biggest acts of love can be to give someone permission to stay away.

Another way of being nice to your friend is offering to help. Not to be "shadow host" as described in the chapter on hygge, but to help reduce stress in different ways. Offer to babysit children or pets or drive your friend to an event. If you are both invited, suggest that you be the one who has to leave early because you're "not feeling well," letting your friend take you home.

Normally, we try to tell the truth, but little white lies are okay in the service of getting some more time to relax in a crazy month. And they are especially allowed when you're helping someone you care about save face and not always be "the sick one."

And who knows… it might help you keep it reasonable for yourself as well.

Chronic Christmas

December 12th
Cut Down on Gifts

Every year, my family agrees to limit gift-giving and, most of the time, we even establish a maximum spending limit. And every year, we all go over. By the time Christmas Eve rolls around – which is when we celebrate – we look at the piles of presents under the tree, shake our heads, and mutter something about "weren't we supposed to go easy this year?"

The problem is, we all love to give presents. And there are kids who need spoiling.

But like everyone else, there are times when the feeling that we *should* be giving a gift to someone takes over. That usually results in buying something generic instead of a gift that is thoughtful and right for the person. We all know those gifts. We get them as well. Those gifts usually end up being recycled or buried in a closet somewhere.

And they're a complete waste of time and money.

Instead, why not find the line between the gifts you want to give (and can afford) and the gifts you're giving because you feel obligated. Make your list and check it twice and, by the end, hope it's been winnowed down to a more reasonable number of people. I'll talk more about this part of gift-giving – or rather, not gift-giving – on December 15th.

Once you have an amended list, talk to the people with whom you exchange gifts about limiting the cost. There are several different ways to do this:

- Some families practice Secret Santa, with or without secrecy. You all pick names out of a hat, so each member of the family only buys presents for one person.
- My mother's family only gave gifts to the kids. Once you hit 18, you were considered an adult and didn't get presents.
- Limit gifts to $20 or less (*such* a challenge and often fun).
- Donate money to your favorite cause instead of buying gifts.
- And according to scuttlebutt, the British Royal family only gives each other joke gifts. Because let's face it, they have pretty much everything.

Cutting down on the number and cost of gifts you give is good for your health. It means less stress and running around. Christmas is about being together with the people you love. It's about hygge.

Because like the Grinch said in my favorite moment from my favorite Christmas cartoon, *Christmas doesn't come from a store.*

20 Gifts under $20

So, you and your friends or family have accepted the challenge to limit the cost of presents to $20 or less. Or maybe you're part of a Secret Santa exchange. Now what do you do? How do you find something inexpensive that is still meaningful?

It is possible. Here are some suggestions:

1. A gift certificate to Amazon, Etsy, the mall, or your local movie theatre.

2. Personalized gift certificates that you create yourself, with offers of specific services you can provide.

3. A small box of particularly delicious chocolates. Note: make sure these are not a trigger for the recipient's chronic illness.

4. A funny mug.

5. Nifty socks. There are all sorts of socks with interesting and funny designs out there. Great for people who like to stand out from the crowd.

6. A coloring book. These are all the rage as stress relief, and they work. Add some coloring pencils as well, depending on the price.

7. A good book (see December 18th for suggestions).

8. A cookbook of easy meals.

9. Aromatherapy, such as essential oils or scented candles. Note: some people are scent sensitive. Make sure you're not giving a gift that will cause a migraine or asthma attack.

10. A tea infuser. These come in all sorts of funny shapes, such as a person basking in a hot tub, a deep-sea diver, a shark, a lollipop, and more. If the price allows, add some loose-leaf tea.

11. Wordy refrigerator magnets. You can get these to spell out poetry, Shakespeare's sonnets, a Scrabble game, and more.

12. A DVD of a great movie, maybe something that is meaningful to the two of you.

13. A T-shirt with a humorous theme.

14. A warm scarf, either knit or pashmina-like. If you like to knit or crochet, something you make yourself is a great idea.

15. A picture frame with a meaningful photo. For instance: grandkids, a beloved dog, the two of you.

16. The perfect notebook.

17. Luxurious soap or lotion. Note: again, make sure the person isn't scent sensitive.

18. Star Wars light-up chopsticks for your favorite geek. They look like small lightsabers!

19. A comic book. Or shall we call it a graphic novel?

20. For the gardeners, a collection of plants and vegetable seeds.

You can find more suggestions by simply Googling "gifts under $20."

Helping Someone with a Chronic Illness

Don't we all have enough stuff? Think about it... Do you really, truly need another knickknack or box of chocolates? Want, sure. Need? Not so much.

So many of us find ourselves overbuying during the holidays, every year ratcheting up the amount of money we spend on each other. The stores want us to spend, spend, spend, and every year, commercials trying to get us to do just that get more outlandish. And really, unless someone you care about can't afford to buy a new recliner or television after the old one gave up the ghost, isn't it a bit nutty to spend that much money on a gift?

Focusing in on what the season is about – love, togetherness, supporting each other – can make the holidays so much more meaningful and less stressful for all of us. Making gift-giving easier and less expensive is one way to do that. I listed several options in the section above.

Obviously, what you do should fit the person and the group. In my opinion, children should have gifts. They may be too little to understand why there are no presents when all their friends get heaps of toys. But it probably wouldn't hurt to cut down on the number of gifts they get. No one needs a mountain of new toys every Christmas.

Another way to adapt this principle is to consider whether there are people in your gift-giving circle who live on fixed incomes. This could be your friend with the chronic illness who may be spending all their money on doctors' appointments and medication. Maybe it would be a kindness to give them something a bit luxurious and frivolous that they wouldn't – couldn't – buy themselves. Or maybe what they truly need is a book of homemade coupons for help over the year, such as a

53

drive to an appointment, a meal for the freezer, and so on. Just make sure you don't forget about honoring the coupons and actually deliver on the promises.

December 13th
Bake a Cookie

One of the themes in this book is the abundance of the holidays, another is being reasonable and pushing back against overindulgence. And today, we're talking about cookies.

There is no such thing as a bad cookie, right? So why not bake seventeen different varieties for Christmas? Most of us completely see the logic in this. After all, according to the media, December is officially cookie month.

This is the time of year when we drag out all the extra-delicious recipes that have been handed down for generations. Or that were in a magazine one year and everyone liked them, so now it's tradition that you bake tons of tins for neighbors, your kids' teachers, the pastor in your church, and as an extra gift for everyone in your family.

Cookies are wonderful, but baking them is exhausting.

I'm not going to suggest that you replace all your homemade goodies with store-bought. Traditions are very much part of what makes this season so special. But let's go back to thinking about being reasonable. About making sure that you can enjoy your holiday traditions, be they baking or actually being conscious for Christmas dinner.

So bake one cookie.

I don't mean just one cookie, I mean one kind of cookie. And yes, I know that all seventeen varieties you normally bake are Very Special and Terribly Essential but try to narrow it down.

Write a list of all the cookies you normally bake, then sit down with a pen and a sense of ruthlessness. The opinions of other people don't matter, except possibly those of your kids, so ditch that fancy recipe you found in a magazine. Then comes the cookie that's really complicated, but doesn't really float your boat. Next on the chopping block is the one that's really tasty, but the dough is physically demanding. Bakeries make yummy gingerbread, so do you really have to make it yourself? And so on. Eventually, you'll discover which cookie is The One.

Then make that cookie – maybe do a double batch. Get your kids involved, play carols, and sing along. And take your time. Enjoy every minute of it, even the ache afterwards.

And then enjoy the energy you now have for other things.

Finskbrød Recipe

If you're making only one kind of cookie, make it an easy one. You probably have a recipe or two in your own arsenal, or you can certainly find some on the Internet. If you go the latter route, don't get seduced by the fancy, time-consuming, and beautiful creations that will impress the neighbors and drive you crazy. Instead, go for something simple, easy, and tasty. Often this is shortbread, and it's an excellent choice.

In my family, it's finskbrød.

Directly (if awkwardly) translated, it means Finnish bread, but it's got nothing at all to do with bread. These cookies are much like shortbread, but slightly different. They are little morsels of buttery, airy crispness, and they melt in your mouth.

Each cookie is one or two bites, and it's hard to stop eating them.

They are also an excellent cookie to use when teaching children about baking. Each cookie is perfectly sized for little fingers to dip into the egg wash and sugar/almond mix. I have some lovely memories of helping my mother make these. She made the dough, and I dipped the cookies, before we both arranged them on a greased baking sheet. I also ate a fair bit of the dough, which is safe because it has no eggs.

Why not try something new this year? If you don't like them, put them in a cookie tin with a bow and give them to a neighbor. And then go buy shortbread from a bakery.

A huge thank you to my mother for sharing this recipe.

Ingredients

Cookie:

1 cup salted butter. Leave it out for a few hours so it's soft.

2 cups all-purpose flour.

1/2 cup granulated sugar

Optional: one pinch of hirschhornsalz (see * below)

Topping:

1 egg

3 tbsp chopped raw almonds (not blanched)

2 tbsp coarse white sugar. This is a type of sugar that is more translucent than actually white. The grains almost look like crystals.

*If you live near a German deli, buy some hirschhornsalz, also called baker's salt or hartshorn salt. The cookies are perfectly lovely without it, but it does add a bit of extra airy crispness.

Knead the cookie ingredients into a dough, being careful not to overwork it. My mother initially wrote that you should do this with your hands, but if they hurt, start the process with a pastry cutter and finish with your hands. Or get your spouse, friends, or kids to do it for you!

Divide the dough into several pieces and roll each into "sausages" about 10 inches long and a bit less than an inch wide. Alas, Mom couldn't be more specific about how many pieces – she's made these little morsels of heaven for so long that it's all by feel. Experiment a little. If the individual portions get too large or small, collect them all into one ball and start over. The dough is pretty soft, so it can be therapy for those of us who have arthritis in our hands. But still be careful not to overwork it.

One additional note is that you should not flour the counter surface when you roll the pieces of dough as it makes them harder to shape.

Cut each "sausage" into five equal pieces. The cut should be at an angle, not straight across.

Dip each piece first in an egg wash, then in a mixture of the chopped almonds and coarse sugar. If someone in your family is allergic to eggs, brushing with water or milk works fine as well. Omit almonds if there are nut allergies.

Place on a greased baking sheet, approximately 2 inches apart. Bake at 350°F or 400°F, depending on your oven, until light brown on the edges. Place on a cooling rack until no longer warm.

Enjoy!

Helping Someone with a Chronic Illness

Much of this book is focused on finding the quintessential part of Christmas and eliminating all the extraneous stuff. And it's something that's good for all of us, whether you have a chronic illness or not.

But even if your friend or family member distills everything about this season down to its essentials, there is something that process doesn't do. And that's dealing with the guilt and depression of having to do this. It's one thing when you cut down out of choice, but when it is forced upon you by a body that won't cooperate like it used to, it's a recipe for feeling really crappy.

The fact that you're reading this means that you are a good friend. And a friend who enables a variety of cookies is a terrific friend.

No, I am definitely not suggesting that you should now bake twice as many of seventeen different types of cookies. Instead, what is needed are your organizational and networking skills.

Have you ever heard of a cookie exchange? You invite a group of people to participate and tell everyone to bake one cookie. A good rule of thumb is to bake half a dozen or a dozen cookies per person attending. The amount depends on how easy the recipe is and how much stamina you have. When the day comes, you exchange the baked goods, giving each other that half or whole dozen. And everyone goes home with a variety!

You can get as loose or as structured about this event as you wish. A very basic approach is to tell everyone to bake a cookie, regardless of the recipe. This does run the risk of the group exchanging several varieties of shortbread. You may want to get a bit more organized, although you don't have to go all the way to creating a spreadsheet. Put together a list of who is coming and what they plan to bring. If, for example, you start seeing a preponderance of shortbread, reach out to a few people and suggest that they bake something else.

There is an additional note regarding cookie safety. Make sure you also ask everyone who's attending about allergies in their families. If someone has a serious allergy to, for instance, nuts or peanuts, it will add a bit of a wrinkle. Unless you keep a nut-free kitchen, there is the risk of cross-contamination, which can put someone's life at risk. If there is a peanut or nut allergy, the safe cookies for that family could be assigned to people who practice nut-free cooking. Another option is to buy your contributions from a nut-free bakery or manufacturer. This will ensure that the baked goodies are safe for everyone.

December 14th
Celebrate the Holidays

Christmas is a very popular holiday. In fact, it's not an exaggeration to say that it's dominant in the Western world. It's quite rude when you think of it, the way it has invaded everywhere.

I hope it's obvious that I'm kidding – I have no intention of insulting Christmas. In fact, it's my favorite holiday. Just like you can tease the people you love the most, so I occasionally make affectionate fun of this holiday I love so much.

But Christmas isn't the only holiday that celebrates the coming of the light in the dark of winter (which is my more secular interpretation of things). Hanukkah, the Jewish festival of lights, is observed at some point between late November and late December, changing from year to year. The Hindu festival of lights called Diwali is in the autumn, which can include December. And the winter solstice, celebrated by pagans, is just a week away.

And then there's Festivus, a holiday made famous on the sitcom *Seinfeld*. It's a blend of secular celebration and parody, and it includes the ritual Airing of Grievances.

There is a reason that some try to make the shift to talking about the holidays, rather than just Christmas. It's a way of being polite, of acknowledging the fact that those of us who observe this particular holiday know that others love their celebrations just as much.

Despite this book focusing on a particular tradition, I think it's important that we recognize the other holidays that celebrate light when it is so dark outside. Unless, that is, you live in the southern hemisphere where there's a lot more light and heat. The celebrations are much the same there, just without the woolen socks.

Why not try to participate in other celebrations as well? Find out about the traditions of your neighbors and friends. Taste their holiday food. Look at the excitement on their faces – doesn't it make them look just like you and your kids? Let us together shine the light of unity and joy.

Because isn't that what the holidays are all about?

Helping Someone with a Chronic Illness

Most of the tips I've shared with you in this book have focused on celebrating the holidays in a particular way. Today, we're looking at the other side of making life easier for someone you care about.

Do you celebrate a holiday that isn't Christmas? Why not invite the person who has a chronic illness to the festivities? It can be the big special celebration with the fancy dinner, although that may be too much for your friend. Instead, you may want to include them in the events that lead up to The Big Day. Just as people who celebrate Christmas prepare and enjoy special events throughout the better part of a month, so do you prepare and enjoy the anticipation. Show others how you do it and share treats and stories from your childhood.

An unfortunate part of this time of year is the way certain media and politicians enjoy harping on our differences, widening the divide between people. Fight back by celebrating together. Remember that love and the spirit of the season are the best ways to fight back against the churlish, whether they be Dickens's Scrooge or Dr. Seuss's the Grinch.

But what if you also observe Christmas? There's a good chance it's slightly different than the way your neighbor, cousin, or friend celebrates. For instance, I'm Danish and that means I celebrate on Christmas Eve, as do many other people in mainland Europe. Our way of decorating is somewhat different from the way it's done in North America and England. The food we enjoy during the season is different as well. Including Canadian friends in our traditions has been a joy. Learning about the ways they celebrate their holidays has been fascinating, tasty, and has enhanced our lives.

Opening up our doors to others, literally or metaphorically, is very much a part of the different holiday traditions that are celebrated during this time. They are about togetherness, being kind to others, and reaching out to people who may be alone or isolated. It makes them feel good, and it makes you feel good.

Chronic Christmas

December 15th
Give the Gift of Time

We are halfway through the month and only ten days away from The Big Day. I bet you're exhausted already, aren't you? This is the time when everything starts seeming really real and really soon. You might even say that Christmas is looming like a charcoal shelf cloud promising a bad storm. No longer is it theoretical, it is imminent.

And there's no way you'll get it all done.

No matter whom you talk to at this stage in the game, the common theme is being so wiped that they simply can't enjoy the lead-up to the holidays. It doesn't matter if it's someone who has a chronic illness or a perfectly healthy individual. Everyone is ready for a nap.

And I could wax poetic (okay, more accurately rant) about how ridiculous it is that we have all become so busy that we don't have time to *live*. I'll save that for the post-holiday slump. Instead, I'm going to suggest something that might help.

Give each other the gift of Time.

The gift of Time doesn't come in a box, and it doesn't actually cost anything. In fact, it may save you money. But that's not why you do it. You do it to give someone extra time to catch up on other important tasks or maybe enough time to catch a nap.

To give the gift of Time, simply agree not to exchange gifts. This means you don't have to spend time thinking about what to get the person, then running around trying to find it in the stores. You also don't have to wrap it and then find time to exchange gifts.

You can also give the gift of Time by not getting together for a holiday drink, lunch, or cocktail party. Save it for January, that dark month when nothing fun happens.

Or you can turn the whole thing on its head. For a few years, a friend and I have literally given each other the gift of our time. Instead of exchanging presents, we have dinner together. Nothing fancy, just pizza, a glass of wine, and face time. It can be a blissful interlude in the frenzy, or it can be postponed until January. The point is to spend time together.

Helping Someone Who Has a Chronic Illness

A lot of the suggestions I've made for what you can do to help someone who has a chronic illness require you to go a little out of your way. To give of your time and your effort during a season when there is often very little of either to find. It's been about empathy, about putting someone else's needs ahead of your own, and scheduling another thing for your list.

Today's idea gives you back some of that time and effort. In fact, you might say that the suggestion is a gift you give yourself.

Giving each other the gift of Time is one of the most precious things you can do for someone you care about. It removes obligation, responsibility, and guilt. And for someone who has a chronic illness, it could be the difference between staying on the couch in pain and having a moment to take care of themselves or do something else that isn't optional.

And it does the same for you. It gives you time to talk to your spouse over a cup of something delicious, run a much-needed errand, or wrap presents early.

Did you like my suggestion above about giving each other your time to be together? It could be argued that most of my Advent ideas have found a way to do just that: allow you to help your friend or family member, sure, but secondly, enable the person to receive help while spending some valuable time together.

There are similarities, but this is just slightly different. This is about giving each other your time, your full focus, with the specific intention of not getting anything done. Except talking, laughing, and sharing a meal.

It's a much-needed timeout for the two of you. A spa moment, if you will, enabling you to take a breath and recharge.

Chronic Christmas

December 16th
Prepare for Stressful People

We all have them. The family member or acquaintance who tests our patience and ability to stay calm and enjoy the holidays. When they head for you, glass of eggnog in hand and an overly concerned or helpful look on their face, the only thing you want to do is disappear into the floor. Or run screaming for the hills. Which can be difficult if your chronic illness limits your mobility.

That person likely only has your best interests in mind. Of course, it's also possible that they are profoundly self-absorbed. Motivation doesn't really matter. What matters is that we end up pinned in a corner, listening to someone yet again suggesting the miracle cures they heard about at the hairdresser's. Or maybe they tried it for a chronic case of hangnails or read about it on the Internet.

Mentally (or actually) rolling your eyes may feel better temporarily, but it doesn't get you out of that corner. Preparation is key. Spend some time before the event thinking about how you'll deal with the situation. For instance, you could work on a pithy reply like, "I really appreciate you thinking of me, but my doctor and I are confident in our treatment choices."

You can also try a more proactive reply straight from the heart of an advocate. "I don't think your hairdresser knows what my chronic illness really means, so I prepared a factsheet for you to share." (Hand over factsheet.)

And then there is the smart-ass reply. The one that deep in our hearts, we all want to give most of all.

"I tried that and got a terrible case of the farts, and boy, did they stink! Did I tell you about the time when I was in the grocery store and couldn't hold them in? No? Boy, are you in for a treat!" And then you engage in a long-winded (sorry) and detailed story that you've made up especially for the occasion.

Another way to deal with the pin-in-the-corner auntie is to plan an exit strategy ahead of time with a sympathetic member of the family. Establish a signal, and ask them to keep an eye out for you. Then when you send out smoke signals, they'll gracefully extricate you from that corner.

Helping Someone with a Chronic Illness

All right, so there are a lot of stressful people out there. You know them, your friend knows them, and I know them.

There are those who are what *Frank*, a now defunct Canadian satirical magazine, called "moist and garrulous." As in drinking too much at parties and never stopping talking. There's the type for whom social events bring out the need to continue old conflicts. Then there's the one who's sobbing in the bathroom, demanding everyone attend to their drama. And so on.

The worst aspect of parties is being stuck dealing with one of these creatively dysfunctional individuals without the ability to gracefully duck away. But for the person who has a chronic illness, that well-meaning (or possibly obnoxious) person can be more than stressful. When Uncle Richard insists he knows better than the entirety of the medical profession, it can not-so-subtly suggest that maybe your friend is not really sick. And that can be really hard to hear.

The person with the chronic illness is dealing with a lot of issues. Pain, fatigue, disability, isolation, and the ongoing stigma of being sick in a world that's made for healthy people. Your friend gets enough messages that they aren't good enough and certainly doesn't need this in a social situation.

And that's where you can help. For instance, by not inviting that obnoxiously "helpful" person and your friend to the same event. If there's no way around having them at your party (or it's not your party), keep an eye on your friend. If you haven't agreed on an SOS signal, pay attention to when they start getting that drawn look and swoop in like the superhero you are.

Have fun with what you decide to say. There's the polite "do you mind if I borrow Susan for a while?" (assuming that your friend's name is Susan). You can also try suggesting that perhaps it's time to mingle.

If you really want to have fun, you can put on your mommy or daddy voice and say, "Now, Uncle Dick, don't you think that Susan has enough on her plate without your uneducated intervention?"

Because let's face it, that's what we all really want to say.

Chronic Christmas

December 17th
Feed the Animals

Not too far from where I live, there's a park with a bunch of squirrels. Urban squirrels tend to be pretty relaxed around people, and these are especially friendly, often peering at you in hopeful expectation. Because people feed them.

In particular, one man is there daily with a bag of nuts. He calls the squirrels, and they come running towards him. They take the nuts from his hands with their paws, stuff them in their mouths, and hurry away to bury them. And then they come back for more. He knows them all individually and can tell you stories about them and their little personalities. If I weren't allergic to nuts, I'd join him in getting to know the fluffy-tailed wee beasties.

In the northern hemisphere, this is the time of year when it's hard for wildlife to find food. Watching birds fluffing up their feathers to create warmth makes you realize how cold it must be for them. It's heartbreaking to watch the shivering squirrels trying to find the nuts they buried, which are now covered by snow and ice. Living with a chronic illness is hard, but at least I have a bed, groceries in my fridge, and a warm home.

Feed the animals. While nature is dormant, help the wildlife.

Take some time to find out what food is best to give them. For instance, bread may not be the best choice for birds. Most grocery stores sell seeds for wild birds that could be a much more nutritious choice. While you're at the store, visit the bulk aisle and fill up a bag with nuts and peanuts to give to the squirrels.

Taking care of others is an opportunity to get out of your head, away from focusing on your pain and fatigue and all the things you can't do. No one's asking you to adopt your local wildlife – in fact, I bet they prefer that you don't. But making it easier for them to survive during this harsh season is a good deed. And all it takes is a bit of birdseed and some nuts.

Helping Someone with a Chronic Illness

A few winters ago, Toronto was in the grip of ice. I've lived in this city for over thirty years, and it was one of the worst winters I've experienced. Lake Ontario was frozen for four months, and I remember spending a lot of time shivering. Which made my pain worse.

Winter can be very difficult for someone who has a chronic illness. The cold and frequent weather changes can be triggers for pain. And more than that, the weather itself can make it difficult for people who have mobility issues to get outside. It's isolating and does a number on your head.

Getting outside is important, even if it's for a short walk. Getting outside and doing something meaningful is even better.

With all the Christmas-related tasks, plus the potential of added pain and fatigue, there may not be enough energy for your friend with chronic illness to dedicate hours to something meaningful. Ten minutes of feeding birds and squirrels and whatever other urban wildlife you can find can make them feel wonderfully useful. It will warm their hearts and might even bring a welcome dose of laughter.

Winter can also be really hard for the wild critters. During that harsh Toronto winter a few years ago, a lot of waterfowl starved to death because of the thick layer of ice on the lake.

Helping your family member or friend do something good for the local wildlife will help you do something good for multiple creatures. Not only are you lending a hand to get another person outside, but you may also be helping to save some little lives.

Your friend may wish to do the research on what to feed the animals themselves. If they are particularly tired, offer to take on that task for them. Either way, pick up the food on your way to pick up your friend and maybe bring a camera as well. It's going to be a special moment, and having a record of it will please you both.

Chronic Christmas

December 18th
Buy Yourself a Present

You have a list, and you've checked it not twice but a dozen times or more. It's color-coded, carefully organized to keep track of which gifts you bought for whom, who you're still working on, and where the gifts are in the various stages between stuck in the closet in a pile of bags to neatly wrapped and under the tree.

Or is that just me?

Somewhere in this rush to be good to others, you've forgotten about yourself. Much of this Advent calendar has been about reminding you to slow down so you can enjoy the season. It's been about doing less, buying less, and spending time with people you care about. About reducing the consumerism of the season and focusing both inward and outward.

Today isn't about that. You might even say that today is the very opposite of everything that this book has emphasized so far.

Because today is All About You. About forgetting everyone else on your list and focusing on you, you, you. Because today, you're going to get yourself a present!

This is going to be the present you haven't told anyone about when they asked you what was on your wish list. Or maybe the gift that no one thinks you really want, even though you've been dropping hints since July. It could be the one you've wanted for years but haven't received yet. Or maybe it's something practical like a funky kitchen tool or a book that can help you live better with chronic illness.

Who better to buy it for you than yourself? You know exactly what size you take, what color you want, and where you can get a good deal on it. So do it. Keep it a secret. Wrap it up in pretty paper with an extravagant bow and disguise your writing when you put down *from Santa* on the tag. Confuse the heck out of everyone and hug your special gift to your bosom with a contented smile.

Gift Ideas for People with Chronic Illness

People with chronic illness aren't just interested in things related to chronic illness. We are just like everyone else – obsessed with knitting, cooking, or cats, addicted to social media, and voracious readers of science fiction or mysteries. Or any other passion or interest that anyone can have.

However, we also have specific wishes and needs related to chronic illness that can make for excellent gifts. This list will give you some good ideas of what to ask for, buy for yourself, or get for someone else.

Gift Certificates

Gift certificates make for terrific presents, allowing the recipient to get exactly what they want or need in the size or color they want or need. Some examples of places that issue gift certificates include:

- Amazon, for pretty much anything your heart desires.
- Major department stores.

- The local mall.
- Movie theatres. This may be particularly welcome if it comes with some company, a drive to and from the theater, and a bag of popcorn.
- Streaming services, such as Netflix.
- Audible.com for audiobooks. These are really useful for people who find it difficult to hold physical books or who have trouble reading text due to eye problems or headaches.
- Massage therapy.
- Personalized gift certificates you make yourself. These could include certificates for a ride to the doctor, a meal (home-cooked or takeout), washing the car, babysitting, or taking the kids to activities. You get the idea.

Special Delivery

There are all sorts of services that deliver interesting packages, usually once a month for a set period of time. You can get food kits, nuts, fresh vegetables, clothing, chocolate, yarn, coffee, and much more. These kinds of services usually use the words "of the month club." They often include items that are a little luxurious that people might not buy for themselves.

Medication and Pain Treatment

Medication is often extremely expensive and can be a real drain on the budget. A gift certificate to the pharmacy where your friend buys their meds could be very welcome. Note: some medications have to be purchased at a particular pharmacy, depending on the person's insurance. If you're not sure where your family member or friend gets their meds, it may be a good idea to buy a Visa or MasterCard gift certificate instead.

How about pretty or funky pill containers? People with chronic illness may have to cart around medication. Having a pretty (or manly) container that doesn't look medical can help them feel less self-conscious about taking meds in public.

If your family member has a lot of pain, a care package to help manage that pain can be a wonderful idea. It can include ice packs, a heating pad, kinesics tape, a movie or book, and a stuffed animal for comfort. You can also add some nibbles, such as flavored teas, chocolate (unless it's a trigger for chronic illness flares), or some delicious dried fruit.

Books

Didn't I just cover books when I talked about gift certificates for Amazon or Audible? Well, yes, but in a more general sense. There are a lot of books out there that someone with a chronic illness might find particularly useful. Below is a small sampling.

You may also want to do a search on Amazon to find more titles about chronic illness in general, as well as do a search on a specific condition to find books that are particularly relevant. Note: check the reviews before you make a decision. This will help you assess whether the book is the kind you want to read or give as a gift.

The Sound of a Wild Snail Eating by Elisabeth Tova Bailey. This is the story of how a bedridden woman finds a way out of frustration with the help of a small snail. It's a beautiful book.

How to Be Sick: A Buddhist-Inspired Guide for the Chronically Ill and Their Caregivers by Toni Bernhard. She's also written two additional books. They are *How to Live Well with Chronic Pain and Illness: A Mindful Guide* and *How to Wake up: A Buddhist-Inspired Guide to Navigating Joy and Sorrow*. You don't have to be Buddhist to get a lot out of these books – they are commonly mentioned in the chronic illness community as being tremendously helpful in learning how to cope.

Strong at the Broken Places: Voices of Illness, a Chorus of Hope by Richard M. Cohen. Through interviews with five people, this wonderful and thought-provoking book explores the world of chronic illness. Cohen has also written *Blindsided: Lifting a Life Above Illness: A Reluctant Memoir.*

Why Does Mommy Hurt?: Helping Children Cope with the Challenges of Having a Caregiver with Chronic Pain, Fibromyalgia, or Autoimmune Disease by Elizabeth M. Christy. This is a fantastic little book for parents or grandparents to help the children in their lives understand chronic illness and pain.

Laugh, Sing, and Eat Like a Pig: How an Empowered Patient Beat Stage IV Cancer (And What Healthcare Can Learn from It) by Dave deBronkart. Not just for people who have cancer, this book is an inspiration to become more empowered.

Chronic Resilience: 10 Sanity-Saving Strategies for Women Coping with the Stress of Illness by Danea Horn. This book has lots of terrific information and exercises. It can also be really helpful for anyone who has a lot of stress.

Mindfulness for Beginners by Jon Kabat-Zinn, PhD. This is a terrific short audio program teaching the basics of mindfulness, which can be a wonderful coping technique for people with chronic illness. The author has also written a number of other books on coping with chronic illness. One of the more commonly referenced is *Full Catastrophe Living: Using the Wisdom of Your Body and Mind to Face Stress, Pain, and Illness*.

Battle for Grace: A Memoir of Pain, Redemption and Impossible Love by Cynthia Toussaint. This is a heartbreaking and beautiful book about what happens when your life is hijacked by chronic illness and what it can do to relationships.

Your Life with Rheumatoid Arthritis: Tools for Managing Treatment, Side Effects and Pain by Lene Andersen. This one is specifically for those of you who live with rheumatoid arthritis and yes, I am suggesting my own book! It is a guide to living well with RA, which has been well received by the community. This one is the first in a series of three books.

Helping Someone with a Chronic Illness

A big part of being a good friend, whether it's to someone to whom you're not related or someone to whom you are, is paying attention. Looking closely enables you to see when they need an ear, a laugh, or just a hug. It's how we nurture relationships. It takes time and effort, but a good relationship is worth it.

Paying attention also enables you to excel at giving gifts. Chances are you have a good idea what this person you care about needs and wants. Sometimes, people with chronic illness don't have a lot of money, because in addition to the regular expenses, there are also a lot of medical bills. They may struggle with guilt about needing to spend so much of the family income on medications and doctors, so they don't spend money on themselves. Or maybe it's just that like almost everyone else, they're not very good at putting themselves first.

So why not get them that gift they won't – or can't – buy for themselves? Buy something that's a bit of a luxury, something that will help them take care of themselves, or maybe something practical that they haven't been able to afford. If you're gifting them something edible, make sure you know what their allergies and potential chronic illness triggers are so you can avoid them.

Receiving a gift has a tendency to make us feel beholden, as if we owe a gift in return. Today's idea is about being a little sneaky, as well as generous. The kind of generosity that takes away any obligation.

So wrap up your present in pretty paper with an extravagant bow, and disguise your writing when you put down *from Santa* on the tag. Confuse the heck out of everyone, particularly that special person, and hold their bewildered joy in your heart with a contented smile.

Chronic Christmas

December 19th
Be Kind to Others

Christmas doesn't come from a store.

Yes, we're back to that immortal sentiment of the green guy in my favorite Christmas special. The journey the Grinch takes from unlovable curmudgeon to full-on Christmas fanatic is funny and heart-warming. Every year there is a certain point when I get disgusted with the constant commercials telling me to buy-buy-buy my way to a happy Christmas. And then I watch *How the Grinch Stole Christmas*. It's only a short cartoon but ever so satisfying. And by the end, my smile is as goofy as that on the face of Max the dog.

Contrary to everything in every commercial, this season isn't actually about spending money. It isn't even about getting presents for each other (or yourself).

This season is about being good to each other, about joy, and about loving your neighbor. One of the most satisfying ways of showing that love and joy is by being kind to each other, including people you don't know. You could argue that it is especially about showing love towards others when it's a bit difficult, and regardless of what they look like, what they do, or when they last took a bath.

Some people like to practice random acts of kindness as they move about their days. You could pay for the coffee of the person behind you at the coffee shop. While you're at it, get a bagel and something hot to drink for the homeless guy out on the sidewalk. Send a letter to a soldier overseas. Have a chat and share a smile with a busy sales clerk in a department store.

You could also leapfrog off our earlier discussion and talk to your family about alternate ways of showing the spirit of the season. Instead of spending money on gifts, volunteer as a family at a homeless shelter or hospital. Perhaps send the money you would have spent on gifts to a worthy cause. Or if exchanging gifts is important (and there's nothing wrong with that), by all means do, but consider adding that donation to the gift budget.

Being nice to other people doesn't just make their day. It makes yours as well. Watching a person's eyes light up with the unexpected delight of being the focus of someone's kind act warms your heart, all the way into tomorrow and the next day.

Helping Someone with a Chronic Illness

If you've made it this far and haven't just read each chapter, but actually followed through on some of the ideas, you have already done something good for someone. Maybe even several someones.

But why stop there?

In addition to all the things you can do to make life easier for that person who has a chronic illness, you can also help them make life easier for someone else.

It can be as simple as being the person to start the discussion about redirecting some of your Christmas budget to a worthy cause. Or you can research volunteer opportunities in your area and put together a list to share with your friend or family member who lives with chronic illness. Suggest you do it together, or offer to act as a chauffeur to and from wherever they want to donate their time and energy.

As you sift potential opportunities, keep in mind that chronic illnesses can be unpredictable. Committing to a specific time, such as Christmas Day, can set you up for failure if the person you care about wakes up in a lot of pain. It's a good idea to find something flexible or an opportunity that they or the two of you can do from home.

Let me share a couple of examples of what's flexible. You can go to the grocery store and shop for a Christmas meal that you donate to your local food bank. Somewhere in your area, a charity will be collecting new, unwrapped toys to give to children at shelters or those who are hospitalized over the holidays.

If the person you're helping has trouble getting out of the house, writing letters can be a wonderful option. Sending someone your warm wishes and gratitude is always welcome. Think about writing a letter to a soldier overseas, a response from Santa to a child, or a note to a past teacher, employer, or someone else who made a difference.

And that's just the start. There are many other things you can do to help someone be good to someone else. Open up the discussion. The two of you will find something that'll mean the world to you both and to the people to whom you give your time.

Chronic Christmas

December 20th
Ask for Help

Me do it.

I'm not a toddler, but you will quite frequently hear me say similar words. Perhaps a bit more eloquently, as my language skills have improved somewhat since I was two. But really. It boils down to the same thing.

I bet you've been stuck in the same place more than once. So often with chronic illness, you need help with doing both big and small things. Like asking your second-grader to help you open the lid on the strawberry jam so you can make their toast. It changes your idea of who you are. And that can get you stuck in a place where you stubbornly insist on doing the things you can't really do, often to your detriment.

But let's not dwell too much on how we may be stuck doing something that's counterproductive to feeling better. Instead, let's talk about ways to break out of it.

Asking for help in general is always a good thing but especially so during this busy month. Yes, I know you hate the idea, but do yourself and your family a favor. Don't do it all on your own. Because that's a recipe for wrecking Christmas.

Let's take a big one: Christmas dinner. Why not invite the family to help you cook? Or start a new Christmas tradition: the potluck dinner. Or, craziest of all, go to a restaurant on the 25th and pay other people to cook the turkey. Or the teriyaki or the Tibetan food – why not try something new?

And it keeps going. Any last-minute errands? Give them to your spouse, your friend, your neighbor. Delegate the decorating of the tree to the kids. My sister and I were assigned this task for years, and it created some lovely memories. When your children are done and call you in to see the magic, be like my mother. Every year, she exclaimed that it was the most beautiful tree we'd ever had. She meant it, too.

Asking for help isn't just something to do so you can enjoy the holidays. It's a gift of love to the people who care about you. Often they feel helpless in the face of your disease. Giving them something tangible and practical to do helps them feel better, too.

Helping Someone with a Chronic Illness

But haven't you been helping this person you care about all month? Well, hopefully you have, but in moderation. Not to the extent that you have completely ignored your own preparations and celebrations. You don't want to leave your children sitting around a wizened and undecorated tree while you're giving your all to someone else. That wouldn't be healthy. The goal of this exercise is to add a bit of help to your family member or friend who has a chronic illness, not to exhaust yourself in the process.

Helping someone else ask for help can be a bit complicated. Most people have a lot of trouble asking for a hand when they need it, and this can be a big stumbling block for people with chronic illness. Even if the willingness to ask for help is there, it can be really difficult to identify what is needed. You making some suggestions can get the conversation started. This can include a ride to the doctor, and while you are there, being moral support during the appointment. It can be picking up meds, babysitting the kids when the person you know is flaring, making a double batch of soup when you're cooking for your family and giving them half. Think about what might help you and suggest that.

Another way to implement today's suggestion is to ask for help yourself. There are a couple of ways you can do this.

One is to ask your friends and family members for help with different aspects of your Christmas celebrations. This frees up energy for you to help the person who has a chronic illness. Well, and maybe enjoy some downtime yourself so you can get through the holidays with your own sanity intact.

Also ask your friend or family member with chronic illness to help you. Always being the person who is receiving help can affect the balance in a relationship. It can get really awkward and feel terrible when you're not able to give as well as receive. Find ways they can give back to you. Maybe you help them in practical ways, and they help you with some phone calls, some Internet research, or simply by listening to you when you're having a rough day.

Relationships are reciprocal. Helping others help you can be a gift.

Chronic Christmas

December 21st
Celebrate Disasters

What do you remember from past Christmases – the times everything went according to plan or the moments when imperfection snuck into the celebrations?

We work so hard to make the holidays perfect, but that's not what makes for enduring family legends. You know the type – the ones that get told and retold, with everyone talking over each other, adding details, and laughing together. Those stories always originate in disasters.

One of my favorite memories was the year of the Leaning Tree of Toronto. My father had just put the stand on the tree, which was a beautiful taller-than-usual pine, and we all stood back and admired its gorgeous symmetry. And then this perfect tree slowly, but inexorably, started tilting and eventually fell over. In the end, we got it back upright and decorated, and it looked gorgeous throughout the season. And you could hardly see the several ropes that tied it to a couple of solid pieces of furniture.

Another of my favorite Christmas traditions is that moment at dinner when my mother criticizes some element of the meal. She has always cooked it to perfection, so we're not quite sure why it needs criticizing, but apparently she feels strongly about this. Or maybe she mentions having forgotten to buy the right napkins, or perhaps the silver is not polished quite to her standards. This is also the moment when my sister and I will intone in unison, "*You fucked up again, Mom,*" and everyone falls about laughing. Yes, even my mother. I have forgotten the event that started this tradition, but it is quintessentially my family at Christmas.

Let go of the necessity for perfection. It causes stress and will make you cry when disaster hits. And it will, because life's like that. One year, the tree will tilt. Another, the dog will steal the sausage for the stuffing and later throw up all over the couch. And then there's the Christmas when you turn on the oven to make the Best Meal of the Year, only to find out that the oven has chosen this moment to give up the ghost.

When it all goes wrong, laugh. Because it's not about the stuffing, the tree, or the turkey. It's about being together. And next year and the year after that, carve out special moments to sit down next to each other and immerse yourself in the memories. Tell and retell the story until it is part of the fabric that holds you all together.

Helping Someone with a Chronic Illness

Every year at Christmas, my mother makes the traditional Danish Christmas dessert ris a la mande. And no, that's not proper French, but it's what the Danes call it. The Canadians in our family call it rice pudding, but no rice pudding is as good as ris a la mande. It involves rice, milk, cream, chopped almonds, and a lot of Madeira. In my family, it is served with a delicious sauce made of black cherries. We believe it's heresy to serve the sauce any other way but cold, but I've heard of other families who use warm cherry sauce or perhaps a strawberry sauce.

Making the cherry sauce is a lengthy process. It starts in August, when I buy five pounds of Bing cherries from British

Columbia and keep them in my freezer. In November, we get together at my mother's and she supervises the next generation as we make the sauce, a process that takes hours.

Last year things went a little sideways. The thickening agent that we get from Denmark had been changed without us noticing it. We put in as much as we usually use, but it was a lot more potent. As the sauce was poured through a sieve into jars, what came out on the bottom of the sieve was a cherry-flavored stalactite. That year the ris a la mande was served with chunks of cherry Jell-O.

This one was so good it instantly became an Andersen family legend.

What helped it become a funny story was the fact that there were several of us who made it so. Had one person been responsible for the cherry sauce, it would have been devastating. Instead, it was done as a group who laugh well together. And that's the key to moving on from a disaster.

Be the person who can listen to your friend when they tell you about a catastrophe that will ruin Christmas. Commiserate, comfort, and then find the comedy in it. Make them laugh. Help them see that this will become a much-treasured family memory.

Being backup to help out when disaster strikes can also be a huge help. You don't have to be ready to step in and recreate the perfect dinner, re-knit the socks that the toddler unravelled, or solve any other of the possible calamities. It is just as helpful to coordinate other people coming to the rescue, whether friends and family or individuals who are paid to provide the service. Anything that can ease the stress.

Chronic Christmas

December 22nd
Embrace Good Enough

How much is left on your list? Unless you are one of those incredibly organized people who have all the bows tied and every piece of tinsel polished before Labor Day, chances are you are near hysterics today.

If you stopped right now, how would it feel? Would you go into a tailspin and accuse me of destroying your beautiful Christmas? I don't think so. I suspect there's a part of you that would feel an overwhelming sense of relief.

There are three days left until The Big Day. I know you have a list, but it's not going to happen.

So I'm going to suggest that you let go of the belief that you will finish it all. There simply isn't enough time or energy. I can hear you arguing with me out there, but you know. Deep inside, you know it's over.

So face the fact that you won't get it all done. Surrender to it. Instead, embrace that wonderful state of relaxation called Good Enough. The handmade table decoration isn't done? Grab a clear bowl, and throw some coordinated Christmas decorations into it atop a bunch of tinsel. Did you plan to make a Yule log, but all of you is aching? You can find all sorts of elaborate and delicious desserts in every grocery store out there.

Embracing Good Enough enables you to slow down and enjoy the last few days before the busy holidays. It creates time when you can enjoy some glögg or eggnog (store-bought, natch!) in front of the fire. Or better yet, in front of that channel on the TV with the fireplace. Good Enough gives you time to play a board game or video game with your kids, time to watch *It's a Wonderful Life*, time to let the stress slowly seep out of your body.

So relax. Take a breath. Wherever you are right now is Good Enough.

Helping Someone with a Chronic Illness

Good Enough. What a tantalizing thought.

I don't know anyone who isn't freaking out three days before Christmas. Your friend or family member who has a chronic illness isn't alone – I bet you are, too. And I'll tell you the exact same thing I said to them. It's over. You're not going to get all of it done. And moreover, you don't have to, and neither do they.

However, they might need a bit of help getting to that emotional state of Zen. Having a chronic illness can already make you feel like you're not good enough – not being able to do everything you used to can do that to a person. So join in and help each other embrace the idea of Good Enough.

The decorations are Good Enough, the stash of treats is Good Enough, throwing the remaining unwrapped gifts in gift bags is Good Enough.

Ahh. Doesn't that feel good?

Well, a quick sidetrack. You may need to help your family member get some last-minute supplies to facilitate the Good Enough. This could include some gift bags, the fancy dessert from the grocery store, and a bit of extra tinsel to throw about the holiday table. Because turning down the lamps and letting lit candles reflect in tinsel can be incredibly festive.

It's just a few more errands, but at this stage and with this intention, they can feel delicious. Because you can see the end. This is the last thing you have to do, and then it's nothing but relaxation and togetherness. Can you feel the giggle rising within you as you contemplate celebrating Christmas without being totally drained?

There is power in numbers. With the two of you letting go and telling other semi-hysterical people that you've decided everything is Good Enough just the way it is, you don't look like slackers. In fact, you could look like the only sane people around. And it might just be an inspiration to other people who need to relax before all the celebratory running around that'll happen in just a few days.

You never know. Maybe the two of you could start a movement.

Chronic Christmas

December 23rd
Sing

When is the last time you sang? I mean really belted one out, disappearing into the music and the feeling, without caring about the dogs howling in the neighbourhood and the cracks appearing in your glasses?

OK, so maybe that last part doesn't happen to everyone. Did I ever mention that my sister has attempted to limit my singing to the shower and Christmas?

I sing anyway.

Every year after dinner on the 24th, we gather around the Christmas tree to sing before we open presents. We have a collection of small songbooks of carols from Denmark. As well, everyone picks a favorite English-language carol or song. We sing all of them.

It is joyful and also very, very funny. Half of the attendees don't understand Danish, but they pick their way along phonetically. It is particularly funny whenever someone new joins our Christmas festivities. Looking slightly shell-shocked, they nevertheless do their best with this strange language. Over the years, they find a favorite, even though they still might not understand the words.

Singing is good for you. It exercises your lungs, opens up your chest, and fills your heart and soul. What better time to get started than this season when beautiful carols are everywhere? They are contagious, making you hum along in the grocery store, on the street, and yes, even in the shower.

Yield to the irresistible power of song this season. Don't just hum along – sing along. You know most of these carols by heart from years of repetition, likely even if you don't celebrate Christmas. They connect us to the spiritual side of this time of year, and it works beautifully no matter what religion you practice.

And don't just sing by yourself, in the car, or at home. Sing with others. Is there a group of neighbors who go carolling in the last few days before Christmas? Bundle up and join them. Go to church and sing with everyone else in the congregation. If you're stuck at home, find an album or YouTube video with choral Christmas music – the Mormon Tabernacle Choir is my favorite. Then crank it to eleven and sing along as loudly as you can.

Helping Someone with a Chronic Illness

I don't know anyone who doesn't like to sing. Maybe not in public though, especially those of us who couldn't sing on key if our lives depended on it. Instead, we tend to reserve it for singing along to the car radio or when we are part of a large group.

But sing we do. Music sneaks by logic and reason, right into our bodies, making us tap our toes and drum the nearest surface. Before you know it, you've opened your mouth and are belting right along with the singer.

Finding a way to incorporate that joy this Christmas and beyond will brighten your mood. And it gets even better when you include someone else, like that person you know who has a chronic illness. Living with health problems can be overwhelming and can take over their life, so there isn't room for a lot of joy. Why not help them reconnect to music?

In the section above, I suggested finding a group of neighbors and going carolling with them. Bring along your friend or family member. If it's cold, be aware that this could be a trigger for their chronic illness and perhaps suggest taking the show inside. Find a room in a community centre or a school, or descend upon someone's living room. Those who have instruments and know how to play, even if only a little, can bring them. Someone else can print out carols from the Internet, and everyone can bring a snack.

And then you sing.

Bring your kids of various ages along and encourage them to join in as well. In the beginning they might be a bit self-conscious, especially the teenagers, but they will soon realize that no one's looking at them and join in, loudly, joyfully, and perhaps not entirely on key.

Because that's the point. That even if you can't sing, being part of a group makes you much less self-conscious, no matter your age.

This could become a tradition with neighbors and friends getting together a few days before Christmas to celebrate the joy of singing together. What a nice way to start the holidays!

Chronic Christmas

December 24th
Julehygge or Welcoming the Spirit of Christmas

Today, my family is celebrating Juleaften.

Celebrating what… ?

Juleaften. Which is how you say Christmas Eve in the Danish language, and it sounds more or less like *Yule afthen*. Where I come from, the grand celebration happens tonight with a special dinner and exchanging presents. And it means that today is about disconnecting and decompressing and letting julehygge take over. Remember hygge, the very Danish way of creating happiness that I talked about on December 10th? Julehygge is a special Christmas version of that.

You might call it the spirit of Christmas.

I know some of you are working today, but I also know that on December 24th, a lot of socializing gets tucked in among the moments of work. It's about visiting, chatting, and trying each other's baked goods. It's a perfect way to start letting go of the stress of work and preparing for the holidays, sliding slowly into celebration.

Today is about getting ready for the big night, and letting the big night enter your heart. To open yourself up to the Christmas spirit so you can celebrate the magic, the light, and the love of the season.

Knowing that tomorrow is likely to be a bit intense, be good to yourself today. Good Enough has left the building. Today, it's about accepting that if it hasn't been done by now, it truly ain't gonna get done. Any of it.

So let it go. Shove the mess in a closet, forget about that extra side dish, and let go of the need to iron anything. It'll help you save up some much-needed energy for the next couple of days.

Then do what makes you happy. Have a hot bath, meditate, do some stretches. Pour yourself a glass of wine, a mug of glögg, or a cup of tea. Settle in with some seasonal songs or a classic movie. Follow Santa's progress on the NORAD website (www.noradsanta.org) with the kids or just on your own and feel the excitement start to build. And then go to bed and get a good night's sleep.

Glædelig jul!

(Which is how the Danes say Merry Christmas.)

Helping Someone with a Chronic Illness

Do you celebrate Christmas on the 24th or the 25th? Maybe your traditions are Orthodox and the festivities aren't until January. Or perhaps you don't observe Christmas at all but something else instead. Regardless of what you do, you understand about that last day before The Big Day. And if yours is tomorrow, you really understand about the pressure.

There is a lot of it, especially today. The stress of it all can make anyone as growly as a bear. For your friend or family member who has a chronic illness, the buildup of pressure has the very real potential to flatten them with a flare. This could lead to spending the holidays lying on the couch while everyone else is having fun around them. Or maybe having to cancel their holiday plans entirely.

If you're doing your own battle with carrying the weight of creating a perfect day for your family, you may be tempted to think that you've helped enough this month. And you're probably right. In no way am I suggesting that you help someone at the expense of what you need to do for you and yours.

But just as that person you know and care about could benefit from letting go of all those last-minute tasks that will drain them completely, so could you. Spending a quiet night watching cartoons with your kids, listening to music, or cuddling the dog will do much to center and recharge you. And just like that person you know, you're probably rolling your eyes at me and preparing to stay up until the wee hours to finish those last tasks.

Don't. Help yourself by helping someone else. Call your friend, commiserate about all the things that aren't done, and remind them that it is more important to be part of Christmas than to make it perfect. Feel those words sink into your own mind. Embrace an imperfect Christmas where both of you have enough energy to really enjoy it.

Work together to let the pressure go. And have a good sleep tonight.

Chronic Christmas

December 25th
Enjoy

Just like that, Christmas is here. Every year I'm surprised by how quickly it comes and how quickly it goes by. It's a little like preparing for a wedding – days and weeks of planning and doing, and we burn through it all in a matter of hours.

If you have kids, you were lucky if you got to sleep in until sunrise today. Your morning has likely been a whirlwind of opening presents, trying on new clothes, and looking for batteries for the new toys. If you retain even a small bit of childlike delight about presents, this wasn't just about the kids. It was for you, too.

Being able to connect to that sense of wonder and magic is what gets you through a busy and often emotional day. Remembering back to how you felt as a child. If your childhood experience wasn't ideal, perhaps seeing the excitement in the faces of the children who are part of your Christmas now will make up for it.

With a bit of luck, you'll be able to sneak in a break to have a cup of delicious coffee or tea with your breakfast and do something for yourself. If you're spending that precious time with this book, I'm honored.

And then the day continues.

I hope you'll get to share the day with people you care about, maybe even the person who has followed along in this book and tried to make life a bit easier for you. Christmas Day can get pretty intense and busy, but try to set aside some time to have a quiet moment with that person. Tell them how much it meant to you that they gave you that kind of backup. Tell them in detail and don't worry if it makes you tear up a little. Enjoy the warmth in your heart.

Even if you followed all the tips in this Chronic Christmas Advent calendar, you have likely burned through every bit of energy you had and then some. Take some painkillers if you need to. Use what I call the Fun Filter – that ability you have to ignore pain and fatigue when you're having a good time. Enjoy the celebration. You can crash tonight.

And when you do, know that you're not alone. I'm crashing right along with you, and so is everyone else, chronic illness or not. Thankfully, there is time to relax in the next day or two.

Have yourself a very Merry Christmas. May it be everything you wished.

Helping Someone with a Chronic Illness

Christmas is scheduled for the same day every year, and yet it is always a bit of a surprise when it arrives. How did it get here so soon?

I hope it's a joyful day for you. One that you get to spend with people you care about and who care about you. Maybe one of them is that friend or family member living with chronic illness whom you have been helping in the past month.

Today, help them like you would anyone else. If you're going to be at the same place, suggest picking them up and driving them home. Find them a chair, and offer to bring them a drink or snack if you're up anyway. And spend some quiet time talking to them and to each of the others with whom you're sharing this day.

Today is about togetherness and love. It's not just about giving to others but also to yourself. Stop running around like the proverbial headless chicken and sit down to be part of it all.

Breathe deeply, look around you, and open yourself up. Let in the feelings of warmth, the laughter, and the love. Let them nourish you and help you get over the exhaustion you feel. Or if it's too deep to be overcome, then let those warm feelings wash over you and color your exhaustion with a deep satisfaction with where you are at this moment in time.

Have yourself a very Merry Christmas. May it be everything you wished.

Chronic Christmas

December 31st
Take It Further

If you have been looking for Chapters 26-30, you can stop now. They aren't here. This book follows the tradition of an Advent calendar, covering just the time leading up to Christmas Day.

And then I broke with tradition.

After writing these past twenty-five chapters, I began thinking about what happens next. Do you stop practicing self-care and being reasonable about what you do the minute Christmas is over? Or, if you're a generally healthy person who has been helping someone you care about who has a chronic illness, do you stop helping them on December 26th?

Of course not.

They say that it takes three weeks to create a habit. This book has squeaked you just past that, so you should have at the very least the beginnings of a new habit now.

If you have a chronic illness, you might have a new habit of instinctively looking at tasks with a critical eye, thinking about how you can make them less stressful. Have you been helping someone with a chronic illness prepare for Christmas? Then maybe the instincts that run through your mind are ways to make something easier, for them and for yourself.

Wouldn't it be a shame to waste those wonderful instincts?

I think you can see where this is going. I'm suggesting that you keep doing what you've been doing in the past month.

Today is the last day of the year. The day we make resolutions for the coming year, most of which we promptly break within days. Because creating a new habit is hard. Especially when it involves depriving yourself. Especially when it takes place during a dark and cold month.

But here you are, already in possession of a new habit. Which means that you have already done the hard work of thinking about how you want to change your life and taking action to do so. You're way ahead of the game!

Why not take what you've done this past month and make it a positive and permanent change for your life? This doesn't mean that you who have the chronic illness will never again do too much and spend days paying for it. Just make sure that when you do, the consequences are worth it.

And you who have been helping someone with a chronic illness don't have to give your entire life to the service of others. Just continue what you've been doing this month – helping out in small ways when you can.

You'll have noticed that the 31st has a slightly different style than the rest of the book. This is for both of you at the same time. It's an encouragement to continue asking for and accepting help, as well as extending a helping hand.

And it goes for both of you. If the assistance only goes one way, it plays havoc with your relationship. Support each other, in ways that are unique to you. Give what you can to the person who has a need. Help is always valuable, whether it is practical or emotional or mental. One person may give more of the practical with the other lending an ear or a mental skill. At the end of the day, you're helping each other, caring for each other.

And that's a beautiful thing.

Happy New Year!

Acknowledgements

This Advent calendar has been all about finding ways to help each other. Getting it ready to be a book rather than a series of blog posts was only possible with the help of some truly wonderful people.

Every year for as long as I can remember, my mother Birthe Andersen has made magic throughout December and especially on Christmas Eve. She has taught me what is really important and how to make julehygge so much more than just an idea. Her love and generosity are why she is my best friend and role model.

Janet Tomas isn't just my partner's sister, she is also a friend and a gift in my life. We share conversations on life, the universe, and coping with chronic illness, as well as giggles, podcast and YouTube obsessions, crafting, and food. And she was the getter of spoons when spoons were needed. Janet said brilliant words that made this book come together in my head.

A long time ago, Andrew Allardyce and I tried to collaborate on a book. Alas, that didn't work out, but all these years later something else has. We have been writing very different stories but being able to talk about the process has been a great help. His support through it all has been nothing short of inspiring.

Stacey Savage Simmons started out as a reader and became a friend. Her information about cookie exchanges was life-altering and perfect for this Advent calendar.

Three wonderful women helped make this book as beautiful as it is. Any remaining imperfections are entirely my fault.

Aimee Coveney of Author Design Studio designed an amazing cover and was nothing but tolerant of a frazzled author on a very tight deadline. I could not be happier with the experience and the cover.

Holly Sawchuk of Writer Rescue did another amazing copy edit and this time while wrangling her champion baby. You can do no better if you are looking for an editor.

And then there's my darling sister Janne "Eagle Eye" Andersen. She took time between a full-time job and raising twins to proofread the final manuscript. This is just another reason why she is the bestest.

Lastly and always, David Govoni. My love, my rock, my partner in adventure. For everything you are and everything you do. Because of you, I fly higher.

About the Author

Lene Andersen is a writer, health and disability advocate, and photographer. She's had rheumatoid arthritis since early childhood, accumulating a half-century of living with chronic illness. Lene lives in Toronto, close to the lake, and shares her home with a cat and too many books. Some of these she wrote herself, including:

Your Life with Rheumatoid Arthritis: Tools for Managing Treatment, Side Effects and Pain

7 Facets: A Meditation on Pain

An author can't succeed without word-of-mouth. If you liked this book, please tell your friends and consider reviewing it on Amazon. Even a short review can make a big difference.

Visit Lene's award-winning blog TheSeatedView.com where she writes about life with rheumatoid arthritis, chronic pain, and disability and shares her passion for photography. She's @theseatedview on Twitter and Instagram, and on Facebook, go to www.facebook.com/LeneAndersenwriter. You can also send Lene an email at lene@yourlifewithra.com.

If you want to be notified when Lene's next book comes out and receive other news, sign up for her almost-monthly newsletter. You can find the sign-up button on TheSeatedView.com or her Facebook page. Your email will never be shared with anyone, and you can unsubscribe anytime.

Made in the USA
San Bernardino, CA
28 November 2016